THIMBLEBERRIES®

Finishing Touches

for

Christmas

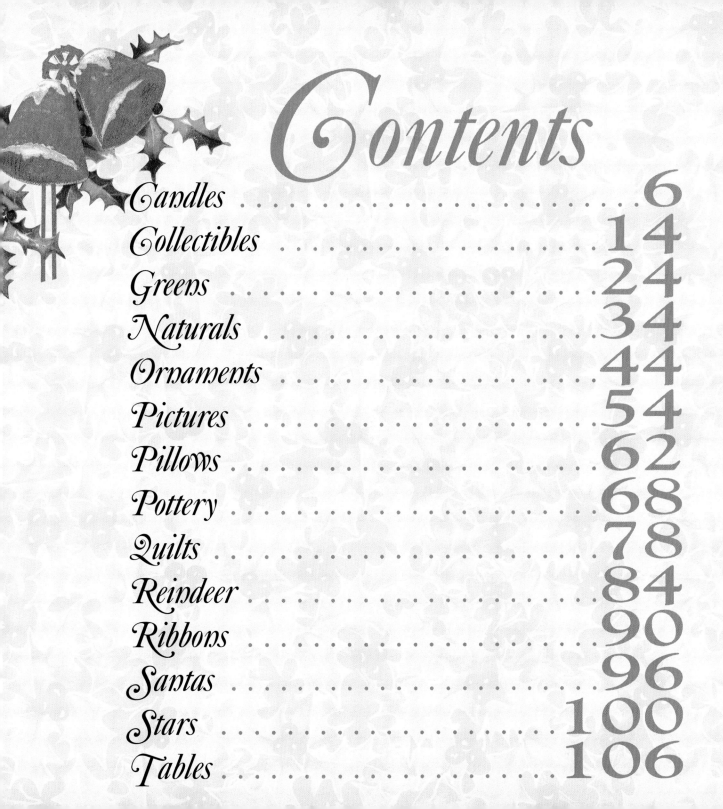

Contents

This book was designed, produced, and published by Landauer Books
A division of Landauer Corporation
12251 Maffitt Road, Cumming, Iowa 50061

President: Jeramy Lanigan Landauer
Vice President: Becky Johnston
Managing Editor: Marlene Hemberger Heuertz
Art Director: Laurel Albright
Creative Director: Lynette Jensen
Photography: Craig Anderson and Amy Cooper
Photostyling: Lynette Jensen and Margaret Sindelar
Technical Writer: Sue Bahr
Graphic Technician: Stewart Cott
Technical Illustrator: Lisa Kirchoff

We also wish to thank the support staff of the Thimbleberries® Design Studio:
Sherry Husske, Virginia Brodd, Renae Ashwill, Ardelle Paulson, Kathy Lobeck,
Carla Plowman, Julie Jergens, Pearl Baysinger, Tracy Schrantz, Leone Rusch, and Julie Borg.
Also, Suzanne Maki for decorative painting and Sue Graff for window treatments.

Printed in USA 10 9 8 7 6 5 4 3 2 1
Library of Congress Cataloging-in-Publication Data available upon request.

ISBN: 1-890621-28-5

Introduction

As the holidays approach,
I have visions of filling the entire
house with finishing touches that
transform my everyday furnishings
to special holiday accessories.
I hope that my ideas for using simple
materials—from candles and collectibles
to pictures and pillows—will inspire
you to add a holiday touch to every
room of your house. With all best
wishes for making your holidays
a time to remember—
especially the finishing touches!

Lynette Jensen

Finishing Touches
Candles

Set the scene for the holidays with a table-top display softly accented by the glow of candlelight. Simply tuck a tiny votive into a cream pitcher nestled in a bed of greens.

Finishing Touches
Candles

For an easy tabletop accent,
bundle cream-colored candles with
an antique postcard tied with narrow ribbon.
Or, place a wreath on a large inverted bowl.
Rest a smaller bowl inside the wreath
to hold a glass chimney filled with a candle
surrounded by miniature apples.

Finishing Touches
Candles

For glowing luminaria wrap rice paper around the outside of a glass chimney or fill the inside of a canister with candles and add simple snowmen stencils to the outside.

Finishing Touches
Candles

Grace the mantel with a trio of candlesticks
filled with white candles and add a trimming
of greens. The antique star is covered with
red chenille roping. Or, surround candles with
holiday fragrance from clove-studded oranges
topped with cinammon sticks.

Finishing Touches
Collectibles

Make your Christmas collectibles the finishing
touches for all the rooms in your house.
Here, bookcase shelves trimmed with paper icicles offer
a wall-to-wall opportunity to show off a collection of
everything from antique books to boxes.

Finishing Touches
Collectibles

Give star attraction to collections of almost anything—
from stockings and stars to plates—
by grouping them for greater impact.

Finishing Touches
Collectibles

Brighten a corner with mounted shelves or a
storage partition on the top of a desk.
Fill them with a collection of miniature bottle
brush trees, houses, and cast iron animals.

Finishing Touches

Collectibles

Choose a theme and carry it throughout
your holiday decorating scheme. Here, the
theme is featured in a large single display of
a vintage house and repeated in a basket
filled with antique house ornaments.

Finishing Touches
Collectibles

For a finishing touch of red and green,
fill a pan painted red with a forest of bottle
brush trees, or display a special tree on
a shelf with a collection of antique toys.

Finishing Touches
Greens

Finding unique ways to display holiday
greens can stretch the imagination—
right up to the rafters! Here, an ornate
porch overhang gets a festive finishing touch.

Finishing Touches
Greens

Tie a few greens to the top of a twig chair, or gather them by the wagonload to add color and interest to the outdoor landscape throughout the holiday season.

Finishing Touches
Greens

Make holiday spirits bright with red, white,
and blue stockings and a mix of trailing greens.
Or, red and green can go outdoors with
an old painted bushel basket bursting with greens.

Finishing Touches
Greens

Finishing touches can be small or large.
A vintage mailbox is home to a handful of greens
and a single pine cone, while the front windows
get dressed with a center swag and garland of
evergreens twined with grapevine and pine cones.

Finishing Touches
Greens

While tiny trees may be finishing touches themselves,
they are host to more decorating details
with branches filled with greens, statice, and mistletoe.

Finishing Touches
Naturals

A fireplace filled with abundance is a sight to behold—naturally! On the wall, a green wreath flocked with a dusting of white is complemented by greenery interspersed with dried hydrangeas and sugar pine cones arranged on the mantel.

Finishing Touches
Naturals

For fast fixings, fill an appliquéd fabric wall
pocket with dried hydrangeas, greens, and red berries.
Toss a handful of pine cones, dried poinsettia leaves,
and holly leaves onto a pewter plate.

Finishing Touches
Naturals

Package up inviting gifts for guests with red ribbon and a few sprigs of greens. Pull off the "old hat trick" by pressing an antique hat rack into service for a festive display of towels topped off with a garland of greens and pine cones.

Finishing Touches
Naturals

For a natural finishing touch, a carpenter's
tool caddy holds greens, sugar pine cones,
and berries celebrating nature's bounty.
And the front hall comes alive with autumn's
harvest of dried hydrangea blossoms.

Finishing Touches
Naturals

Dried hydrangea blossoms add natural
abundance to a basket bouquet or a tree
loaded with ornaments and collectibles.
The rustic wardrobe swagged with pine
cones sets the scene for a collection of
everything from stockings to snowshoes.

Finishing Touches
Ornaments

Glass ball ornaments make fabulous finishing touches because they are always in style—whether you buy new ones or collect vintage ornaments. As with most collectibles, finding them in the original boxes adds to their value and adds a touch of nostalgia to any display.

Finishing Touches
Ornaments

Small tabletop trees laden with delicate
glass balls in pinks, blues, and yellows transform
any room into a pink-frosted pastel dreamland.

Finishing Touches
Ornaments

A large feather tree easily accommodates
an assortment of prized glass ball ornaments.
For a themed tree, focus on a single style of
ornament such as the glass pine cone collection in
shades of cranberry, blue, and gold shown below.

Finishing Touches
Ornaments

Reminiscent of sugar-frosted gum drops, strings of novelty lights add a touch of whimsy to a snowman-stenciled canister used as a container. It's easy to fill the tree with old-fashioned holiday spirit and summer collectibles. Add unexpected items to a tree such as tin pails and tops for old-fashioned holiday spirit.

Finishing Touches
Ornaments

Woolen house and star ornaments with buttonhole
stitching details are in soft contrast to the brightly
painted papier-maché heart ornaments on the tree.
Edible ornaments such as the wrapped candy canes
appeal to young and old alike.

Finishing Touches
Pictures

An impressive N.C. Wyeth print provides quick visual impact and establishes the Santa theme—literally carried up the stairs by colorfully-wrapped gifts each topped with a papier-maché boot.

Finishing Touches
Pictures

Framed pictures of snow scenes can be anything from cheerful to tranquil—and give the feeling that Christmas is just around the corner.

A Merry Christmas and a Happy New Year

Finishing Touches
Pictures

An antique Christmas postcard swings back into holiday style in an old-fashioned swivel frame. The Santa shown below is a fragile antique ornament from the early 1900's. The ornament floats on a mat. Spacers are then used before the two outer mats are added to give it a dimensional quality.

Finishing Touches
Pictures

Going under glass transforms wool and buttonhole-stitched country village ornaments into unique holiday artwork. In contrast to the often hectic pace of the holidays, framed pastoral prints offer a view of more tranquil times from a bygone era.

Finishing Touches
Pillows

Pillows offer a picture-perfect way to add finishing touches to your holiday decorating. Here, an old-fashioned cottage scene is fast-forwarded to the present with easy embroidery stitches worked on a wool background.

Finishing Touches
Pillows

A three-tiered tree on a single block takes
center stage on a pillow top that works up quickly
for a fast decorating accent. Pillow pals such
as this winsome pair of skating partners from vintage
embroidery are holiday heartwarmers.

Finishing Touches
Pillows

Appliqués like the white woolen snowflakes shown below are easy add-ons to special occasion pillows. The rug-hooked and bow-tied Scotty dog was rescued from vintage black velvet and stitched onto a more pleasing pillow background of nubby textured tan wool.

Finishing Touches
Pottery

Display mixing bowls in a pine cupboard and rearrange them seasonally. At Christmastime, feature Yelloware, and green and caramel bowls brimming with artificial sugar-frosted fruit, pomegranates, and greens interspersed with gingerbread houses, trees, and stars.

Finishing Touches
Pottery

Gather old pottery favorites—from flowerpots to fine china—and display them as finishing touches for the holidays. It's as easy as filling green flowerpots to overflowing with red and white-striped candy canes.

Finishing Touches
Pottery

Mixing greens, holly, and pine cones with pottery collections can transform everyday cupboards into instant holiday attractions. Vintage 1940's Blue Ridge Crab Apple dishes, vases, and flowerpots add a dash of Christmas color.

Finishing Touches
Pottery

Color comes softly with a collection of pastel pottery pieces filled with artificial snow, antique bottle brush trees, and Shiny Bright ornaments. Cranberry, green, and white dishes lend a soft touch to a corner cupboard.

Finishing Touches
Pottery

The real story of finishing touches for Christmas is told in a tale of two teapots. A solo pitcher and a daring duo of red teapots add a festive touch to a year-round collection of blue and white pottery. A pair of white teapots embellished with cranberry flowers complements white stoneware featuring clover accents.

Finishing Touches
Quilts

Coming home to comfort at Christmastime is as easy
as decorating with quilts in every room—especially
the bedroom. Take time to rest, reflect, and refresh in a
safe haven accented with the gentle touch of quilts.

Finishing Touches
Quilts

Nothing highlights a table better than a quilt.
Dress up the holiday dinner table with a
quilted runner. Or, create instant cottage charm with a
vintage dollhouse displayed on a quilt-draped tabletop.

Finishing Touches
Quilts

Whether it'a table set for two or twenty, quilts are a last-minute decorator's delight. A generously-sized antique appliqué quilt dresses up the dessert table, and a vintage quilt pieced to look like a red brick fireplace warms up a casual supper by the fire.

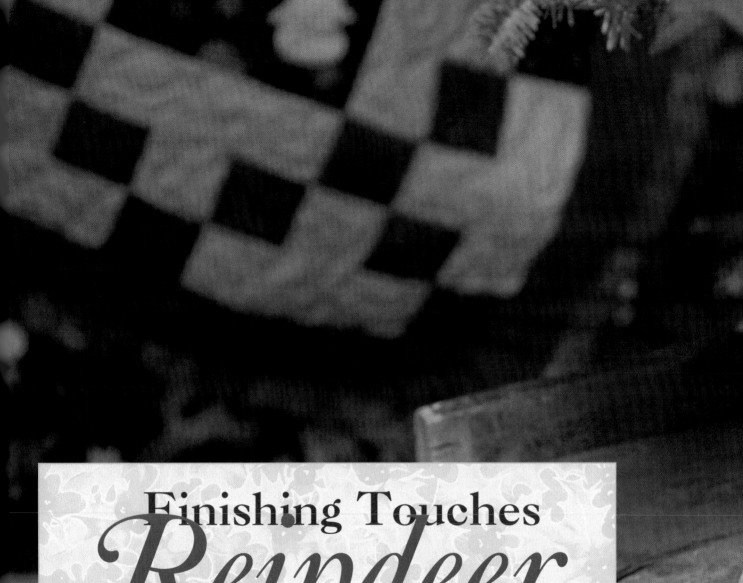

Finishing Touches
Reindeer

Since Santa and his reindeer are synonymous with Christmas, let them spread holiday cheer throughout your home. Here, Santa and his team soar above the rooftops on an antique cone-shaped tree stand.

Finishing Touches
Reindeer

Small but spirited vintage plastic reindeer ornaments prance among tree branches, and fly through the air in a framed antique German die-cut Christmas greeting.

Finishing Touches
Reindeer

Include white celluloid stags in an elegant
tabletop centerpiece, or for a touch of whimsy,
display a vintage 1950 Rudolph the Red Nosed
Reindeer night light nestled with a basket of greens.

Finishing Touches
Ribbons

Keep decorative touches of "gifts to go" on hand for friends and family. Bundle up cookies in star-studded cellophane bags tied with red and green ribbons and nestle them in cups of holiday cheer to go!

Finishing Touches
Ribbons

For a memorable holiday dinner, tie salad plates with sheer gold ribbon trimmed with pine cone ornaments. Or, stack up graduated sizes of star sugar cookies secured with frosting and surrounded with a swirl of ribbon.

Finishing Touches
Ribbons

From muffins to music—tie it all together with a finishing touch of ribbon. Solid or sheer, ribbon adds holiday color to everything from a package trimmed with sheet music to a plate piled high with muffins.

Finishing Touches
Santas

Santas on display offer seasons greetings to one and all. Spread holiday cheer with quickly assembled groupings of your favorite Santas—collect them in wood, resin, porcelain, ceramic or soft sculpture.

Finishing Touches
Santas

From a finely-crafted fabric Santa to vintage
wrapping paper, note cards, gift tags, stickers
and stamps, say it with Santa—Merry Christmas!

Finishing Touches
Stars

It's Christmas Eve and the stars are out
tonight—on beautifully-wrapped packages
and lots of cookies for Santa.

Finishing Touches
Stars

Following the star has never been easier with star-shaped ornaments and gift boxes available in abundance. The tiny 2-inch antique church ornament adds a sparkling touch to a star box lid dusted with glitter.

Finishing Touches
Stars

Finish decorating the table or the mantel
with a sprinkling of stars—from sugar
cookie treats to papier-mache' ornaments.

Finishing Touches

Tables

Finishing touches of sparkling ribbon, stenciled snowflakes, stacked star sugar cookies, quilted runners, and candles all aglow complement each other on a festive table all dressed up in holiday splendor.

Finishing Touches
Tables

Set the table with red, white, and green accents for an early morning breakfast of hearty granola or an elegant after dinner dessert complete with silver coffee service.

Finishing Touches
Tables

Come full circle with a formal dining room
table accented with finishing touches of
white, gold, and, most of all—candlelight.

About Lynette Jensen

Expressing her creativity first through designing quilts, Lynette discovered that by designing her own line of coordinating fabrics she could get exactly what she needed for her growing collection of pieced patchwork.

Known and respected throughout the quilting world for her Thimbleberries® line of fabrics, Lynette has created an enduring collection of coordinates in a rich palette of country colors that literally spans the seasons. Lynette combines traditional quilt patterns with an appealing array of appliquéd vines, berries, and blossoms. The result is a charming blend of blocks and borders with soft touches of country color.

For Lynette, a Minnesota native and graduate of the University of Minnesota with a degree in Home Economics, the Thimbleberries® design studio and office is a short walk from the home she shares with husband Neil. The spacious studio, filled with antiques and quilts, is a wonderful, open, bright spot from which to work and design each day. In this creative setting, Lynette Jensen designs fabrics and quilts and develops classic country decorating themes which express her unique gift for making harmony the heart of the home.